THE CUPBOARD
John Burningham

Jonathan Cape Thirty-two Bedford Square London

There is a cupboard
in our kitchen

It is full
of pots and pans

BREAD

I like
to take them all out

And play with them

Mummy says
why don't I think
of something else
to do

Because I am
in the way

So I think
of something
else to do

But Mummy says
will I please come back

And put all the
things away

Little Books
by John Burningham

THE BABY

THE RABBIT

THE SCHOOL

THE SNOW

THE DOG

THE BLANKET

THE FRIEND

THE CUPBOARD